GREAT & HIDDEN THINGS

THE BOOK OF JEREMIAH
EXPERIENCE GUIDE

PAIR YOUR
EXPERIENCE GUIDE
WITH THE
FIRST 5 MOBILE APP!

This Experience Guide is designed to accompany
your study of Scripture in the First 5 mobile app.
You can use it as a standalone study, or as an
accompanying guide to the daily content
within First 5.

First 5 is a free mobile app developed by
Proverbs 31 Ministries to transform your
daily time with God.

*Go to the app store on your smartphone,
download the First 5 app and create a free account!*

WWW.FIRST5.ORG

HEY FRIENDS,

I'm so excited to welcome you to our study of Jeremiah! Who's cheering with me?

I know, I know. Excited might not be the first word you connect to the study of a major prophet. Prophetical books tend to drum up a more serious tone. We can even approach a book like Jeremiah with some resistance. These books have a reputation for being hard to read, and who wants to be sad all the time?

It's true, in Jeremiah we will walk with God's people through some of the most tumultuous days of their history and follow the prophet through the painstaking task of repeatedly warning an unresponsive crowd.

But in spite of the hostile setting, there are things in this book I'm excited about.

First, we get to trace the steps of the bold prophet, Jeremiah. He told the truth, every single word of it, no matter what the landscape of his listeners presented. And I think we can relate to some of his struggles.

We'll see Jeremiah respond to God even when he feels too young and ill-equipped for his assignment. We'll see what he does in the face of strong opposition to his message of truth. And we'll learn from him as he encounters false prophets.

These issues are not strapped to the life and times of the Old Testament. Years later, in the New Testament, Paul encourages Timothy not to let his young age get in the way of obeying God. (1 Timothy 4:12) He exhorts Timothy to preach boldly and warns him of false witnesses to the truth. (2 Timothy 4:2-5)

If you're like me, you aren't a stranger to feelings of inadequacy to carry out God's assignments and concern about what to do when you face opposition to God's truth.

I'm also excited about the hope woven through the pages of Israelite suffering. In the midst of the hard truth Jeremiah delivered to a people unwilling to yield and return to God, we also find some of the most well-known promises in Scripture.

The pages of Jeremiah span many emotions. From the lowest depths of God's people's sin to the mountaintops of God's promise of our righteous Savior. (Jeremiah 23:6) We might shed some tears and maybe shout for joy before we're finished. But our sin is the greatest backdrop for God's grace.

I expect to absorb truth in this study that will challenge me, bless me, convict me and change me. I'm on the edge of my seat! Are you ready to get started?

Sincerely,

MAJOR MOMENTS OF

jeremiah

THE FOLLOWING IS A LIST OF SOME OF THE MAJOR MOMENTS WITHIN
THE BOOK OF JEREMIAH. CHECK THE BOX AS YOU MEMORIZE EACH ONE.

☐ JEREMIAH 01: *God calls Jeremiah to prophesy to His people.*

☐ JEREMIAH 02: *The Lord is faithful to an unfaithful Israel.*

☐ JEREMIAH 03: *God calls Israel to return to Him and promises healing.*

☐ JEREMIAH 04: *Jeremiah warns of coming judgment by way of a Babylonian invasion and mourns for Israel.*

☐ JEREMIAH 05: *Jeremiah searches for one righteous person in Jerusalem. God cannot tolerate Israel's injustice.*

☐ JEREMIAH 06: *Jeremiah tells the Israelites to flee Jerusalem to escape the coming invasion.*

☐ JEREMIAH 07: *Jeremiah gives a sermon at the temple.*

☐ JEREMIAH 08: *Judgment is coming on Israel because of their faithlessness.*

☐ JEREMIAH 09: *God's goodness requires Him to punish evil.*

☐ JEREMIAH 10: *Jeremiah contrasts false religion with the one true God.*

☐ JEREMIAH 11: *God reminds the Israelites of their covenant.*

☐ JEREMIAH 12: *Jeremiah laments his suffering and God mourns the loss of relationship with His people.*

☐ JEREMIAH 13: *God illustrates His relationship with Judah through the ruined linen loincloth.*

☐ JEREMIAH 14: *Jeremiah prophesies concerning the drought in Judah and Jeremiah attempts to intercede on their behalf.*

☐ JEREMIAH 15: *God refuses to relent. Jeremiah laments his loneliness and God comforts him.*

☐ JEREMIAH 16: *God gives Jeremiah personal directives and promises His people will return to their land.*

☐ JEREMIAH 17: *God describes sin and its consequences and instructs Jeremiah to teach the Sabbath.*

☐ JEREMIAH 18: *A potter works the clay vessel and Jeremiah seeks vengeance.*

☐ JEREMIAH 19: *Jeremiah speaks to the elders at the Valley of the Son of Himmon and renames it the Valley of Slaughter.*

☐ JEREMIAH 20: *Jeremiah is persecuted by Pashhur and laments his situation.*

☐ JEREMIAH 21: *God gives Jeremiah prophecies for the last kings of Judah.*

☐ JEREMIAH 22: *Jeremiah continues with prophecies for the sons of Josiah.*

☐ JEREMIAH 23: *Jeremiah tells of a coming Messiah and condemns the lying prophets.*

☐ JEREMIAH 24: *Jeremiah has a vision about good and bad figs.*

☐ JEREMIAH 25: *Judah has refused to repent after many years of Jeremiah's prophecy. The nations around Judah will also drink the cup of God's wrath.*

MORE MAJOR MOMENTS OF
jeremiah

☐ JEREMIAH 26: *Jeremiah brings every word of God's message despite threats of death.*

☐ JEREMIAH 27: *God has given temporary power to Nebuchadnezzar and calls His people to submit.*

☐ JEREMIAH 28: *Hananiah offers an opposing prophecy and dies as a result.*

☐ JEREMIAH 29: *God sends a message of encouragement to the exiles and a message of judgment to those who refused Babylon's yoke.*

☐ JEREMIAH 30: *Judah and Israel will be restored to God and their land.*

☐ JEREMIAH 31: *A new and better covenant is promised.*

☐ JEREMIAH 32: *God instructs Jeremiah to purchase a field as a sign of promised future restoration.*

☐ JEREMIAH 33: *The Lord promises His people peace and prosperity and that His covenant can never be broken.*

☐ JEREMIAH 34: *Jeremiah prophesies about Zedekiah's future and against Judah's treatment of slaves.*

☐ JEREMIAH 35: *The Rechabites exemplify obedience.*

☐ JEREMIAH 36: *God commands Jeremiah to write a scroll of all of Jeremiah's prophecies to give to Jehoiakim.*

☐ JEREMIAH 37: *Zedekiah questions Jeremiah in prison.*

☐ JEREMIAH 38: *Jeremiah is saved from the cistern and is visited by Zedekiah.*

☐ JEREMIAH 39: *Jerusalem is conquered, Zedekiah is punished for his faithlessness and Ebed-melech is rewarded for his faithfulness.*

☐ JEREMIAH 40: *Jeremiah is released and stays in Judah under Gedaliah.*

☐ JEREMIAH 41: *Ishmael murders Gedaliah and attempts to take the remnant to the Ammonites until Johanan intervenes.*

☐ JEREMIAH 42: *God commands the remnant to stay in Judah where He will bless them.*

☐ JEREMIAH 43: *Johanan and the remnant flee to Egypt to seek safety.*

☐ JEREMIAH 44: *The remnant in Egypt turn to idolatry.*

☐ JEREMIAH 45: *Jeremiah gives Baruch a message.*

☐ JEREMIAH 46: *God promises judgment on Egypt.*

☐ JEREMIAH 47: *God promises judgment on the Philistines.*

☐ JEREMIAH 48: *God promises judgment on Moab.*

☐ JEREMIAH 49: *God promises judgment on Ammon, Edom, Damascus, Kedar, Hadzor and Elam.*

☐ JEREMIAH 50: *God promises judgment on Babylon.*

☐ JEREMIAH 51: *Jeremiah's prophecy of judgment is brought to Babylon.*

☐ JEREMIAH 52: *The fall of Jerusalem is retold.*

WHY EXPERIENCE

jeremiah?

HAVE YOU EVER BEEN IN A POSITION WHERE SOMEONE ASKED YOU TO DO SOMETHING REALLY HARD?

In that moment you might have weighed your options and the potential consequences: What if I just ignored the request and didn't do it? What would happen if I did do it? What would people think of me? How would it impact my life? All of these questions will ultimately lead to two possible responses: Either you do what was asked, or you decide it's not worth it and you don't.

God asked the prophet Jeremiah to do something really hard. God spoke through Jeremiah to give a message to the southern kingdom of Judah, warning them of their wicked behavior, calling them to repent and prophesying the consequences that would await them if they did not return to their God.

Jeremiah covers decades of Judean history and chronicles the last few kings of Judah. At that time, their security and status were under constant threat and they desired to be safe and prosperous in the Promised Land like they had once been. But Jeremiah would be their last prophet before God's people were exiled to Babylon because of their rejection of God.

Why weren't the people of God responsive to the message of Jeremiah? Sadly, the people of Judah had succumbed to deception. (Jeremiah 7:1-15) They were deceived by false gods, false prophets and false words. This deception turned them to the destruction of the fatherless, the orphan and the poor — all those living at the margins of society.

Bearing the image of God, their behavior did not reflect the character of God. The prophet Jeremiah speaks into these circumstances and calls the Israelites to repent and walk in good ways so they might experience the goodness of God. Yet, God's people refuse to live according to His will. (Jeremiah 6:16)

God not only made His current will known through Jeremiah, He also gave Jeremiah a glimpse of the "great and hidden things" to come. (Jeremiah 33:3) These great and hidden things are not only of Judah's destruction, but a promise of a future hope. Jeremiah got a glimpse into God's plan for all of creation. This is the life-giving promise of rescue through the renewal of God's covenant that was first established as a promise to Moses. (Exodus 24:1-8) The first covenant was broken routinely by God's people, yet God promises to write the new covenant upon the hearts of His people and forgive their sins. (Jeremiah 31:31-34)

Jeremiah's prophecies are ultimately realized in the person of Jesus Christ — the great reconciler and salvation for us all. Through Christ we are given the gift of the Holy Spirit who has written the law on our hearts, fulfilling what the prophet Jeremiah prophesied so long ago. (Jeremiah 31:33; Hebrews 10:16; Romans 2:15)

The book of Jeremiah begs us to ask ourselves what God has asked us to do for His kingdom. What call has God asked of us individually? While the execution of the call may look different for everyone, the purpose is the same for the covenant people of God. The Apostle Paul describes it as the ministry of reconciliation. (2 Corinthians 5:18-21) God is making His appeal to humanity through His chosen people.

We are no different. We are just as broken and deceived as the Israelites and Judeans in the time of Jeremiah. We've all been deceived by false promises.

Seeped into the ancient pages of the book of Jeremiah is an immensely applicable example of what it looks like for believers to stay faithful to what God has asked of them. The prophet Jeremiah honored God in his persistence for God's message, even though he was met with opposition and oppression. Our perseverance to fulfill God's call will serve as a sign to a broken humanity that God has all of our affections. The experience of persecution is worth it for the sake of honoring God by calling all people to return to their God.

GETTING TO KNOW
the author

The book of Jeremiah chronicles the messages of the prophet Jeremiah. In the ancient Near East, names were of particular importance and often indicated something about the individual's life and purpose. This is evident when it comes to Jeremiah, whose name consists of two Hebrew words: רום (*rum*: to raise up/establish) and יה (*yh*), which is a shortened form of Yahweh.[1]

Together, his name is translated as "Yahweh has raised up," and this is exactly what the Lord did. Yahweh calls Jeremiah while still in his youth, during the reign of King Josiah (Jeremiah 1:2, 6), and sets him on a journey filled with challenge and opposition.

As we look at the books of Jeremiah, 1 and 2 Kings and 1 and 2 Chronicles, we gain more information about Jeremiah than any other prophet. We know he was born in the seventh century B.C. in an important town called Anathoth, three miles northeast of the city of Jerusalem. King Solomon banished the high priest Abiathar to Anathoth decades earlier (1 Kings 2:26), leading some scholars to believe that Abiathar could have been a relative of Jeremiah, placing him in a family of high priests.

Jeremiah is one of three major prophets, along with Isaiah and Ezekiel. These books are called "major" because of how much larger they are in comparison to the other prophetic books.

Jeremiah is often referred to as the "weeping prophet" because he spends his life speaking to a stubborn and unrepentant Israel, continuously mourning their destruction. Jeremiah is forced to watch the people he loves be subjected to oppression and sent into exile as a result of their refusal to heed the warning of the Lord.

Traditionally the book of Lamentations is also said to be written by Jeremiah. Lamentations was written after the destruction of Jerusalem and during the Babylonian exile — right where Jeremiah leaves off. Although Lamentations officially remains anonymous, there is too much overlap between Jeremiah and Lamentations to ignore the probability that Jeremiah authored both.

Jeremiah was well accustomed to persecution and opposition from average people and royalty alike. We see this in Jeremiah 36 where King Jehoiakim burns one of Jeremiah's scrolls as a sign of contempt and opposition. Because of his great persecution, possibly one of the greatest things we can learn from Jeremiah is his steadfast and persistent nature. We will see Jeremiah become agitated, depressed and fearful, but he was committed to communicating the message God gave him despite his own personal pain and doubt. He continued to be faithful to the message God gave him, never wavering from God's great and glorious truth.

[1] Heyink, Brenda. "Jeremiah the Prophet." Edited by John D. Barry, David Bomar, Derek R. Brown, Rachel Klippenstein, Douglas Mangum, Carrie Sinclair Wolcott, Lazarus Wentz, Elliot Ritzema, and Wendy Widder. *The Lexham Bible Dictionary*. Bellingham, WA: Lexham Press, 2016.

COMMUNITY AND
culture

The book of Jeremiah is particularly special in light of the wealth of historical information we are given about what Judah was like at that time. Jeremiah prophesies almost exclusively to Judah — the southern kingdom that remained after Israel pursued idolatry. (1 Kings 11-12) The people of Judah had seen how the Assyrians destroyed and took the northern kingdom of Israel into exile. Judah received countless refugees from the northern kingdom who fled Assyrian captivity.

Judah found themselves at the tipping point of their history. During the days of Jeremiah, they experienced fleeting moments of prosperity that were finally met with persecution and imprisonment from the Babylonians.

Judah's short-lived prosperity was tied directly to Assyria's conquest of Israel and other political and military exploits, leaving Judah at peace for a time. It was around then that the last righteous ruler of Judah, King Josiah, began his reform. Josiah redirected tribute money he had been required to send to Assyria to begin repairs of the temple. It was during these repairs that the Book of the Law was found. Josiah responded by tearing down the high places and leading Judah back to their God through genuine repentance and reform. (2 Kings 22:1-23:3)

Sadly, this reform and renewal was short-lived after Josiah died in battle near Megiddo. (2 Kings 23:29-30) Judah quickly came under the control of the Egyptians, who then lost their power to the devastating military might of Babylon. In one fell swoop, Babylon replaced Assyria and Egypt as the superpower in the ancient world. As a result of the Babylonian threat, Jehoiakim (who was placed as king of Judah by the Egyptians prior to the Egyptian fall) allowed idolatry, social oppression and wickedness to come back in full force — all of the things his father, Josiah, worked so hard to undo.

Jeremiah prophesies and delivers his message to the people of Judah who now find themselves in this turmoil. Their community has continuously been sent into upheaval by the leading superpowers of the time. Their culture was being transformed to reflect the pagan and idolatrous values of these conquering superpowers, rather than resembling and reflecting the covenant relationship they were marked by as the children of God.

These 40 years of instability through five Judean kings could have been an opportunity for the people to cling to God, but instead they hoped in what they could see tangibly. Jeremiah was present through it all, from the reforms of Josiah, to the Babylonian exile, steadily proclaiming the word of God.

UNIQUELY
jeremiah

AS MENTIONED in the community and culture section, one of the unique aspects of Jeremiah is how much we know about this prophet, his ministry and the people of Judah from other books of the Bible. We can turn to the books of 1 and 2 Kings and 1 and 2 Chronicles to learn about the historical, cultural, social and political settings of not only the kingdoms of Israel and Judah, but the landscape of the entire ancient middle eastern world. Yet, with as much as we can learn externally, we can also learn from the book of Jeremiah itself. The book of Jeremiah is around 42,000 words and of the three major prophets (Isaiah, Jeremiah, Ezekiel) Jeremiah is not only the longest major prophet book, but it is the longest single book in the entire Bible!

As well as the length, the structure of the book is unique. For example, half of Jeremiah is poetic in nature while the other half is prose. This moves us between storytelling, reflective poems and prophecies. As we read Jeremiah, pay close attention to the particular form and method of writing of each section. When we can identify the type of writing we are studying, we can more accurately interpret and apply the book of Jeremiah because it will indicate if it is a literal story of what is happening at the time, a future prophecy that we can connect with other Scripture or a poem that uses imagery.

Jeremiah 11:18-21 is an example of poetic structure used by Jeremiah.

JEREMIAH 11:19 SAYS:

> But I was like a gentle lamb
> led to the slaughter.
> I did not know it was against me
> they devised schemes, saying,
> "Let us destroy the tree with its fruit,
> let us cut him off from the land of the living,
> that his name be remembered no more."

Jeremiah is describing his own personal experience, yet these words also bring to mind the reality of the greater prophet, Jesus. Jesus was also like a gentle lamb who was led to the slaughter while the Pharisees and Sadducees devised schemes against him. Finally, this leads us to the important connection of the suffering and oppression of Jeremiah. Jeremiah's suffering (Jeremiah 15:10-12; 20:1-2, 7-18; 26:7-24) is a critical theme that connects him directly to the suffering of Christ Himself. Our reading of Jeremiah is important in our understanding of what it looks like to be a suffering servant of the Lord.

The book of Jeremiah is rich, but can seem complicated. At first glance the narrative seems hard to follow because it is not all in chronological order and the sheer length of the book can be daunting. As we read together you will also notice that the book covers a lot of different themes! But hang in there with us because God's truth is woven beautifully throughout Jeremiah. God had a lot to say through Jeremiah to His people then and He has a lot to say through Jeremiah to us now.

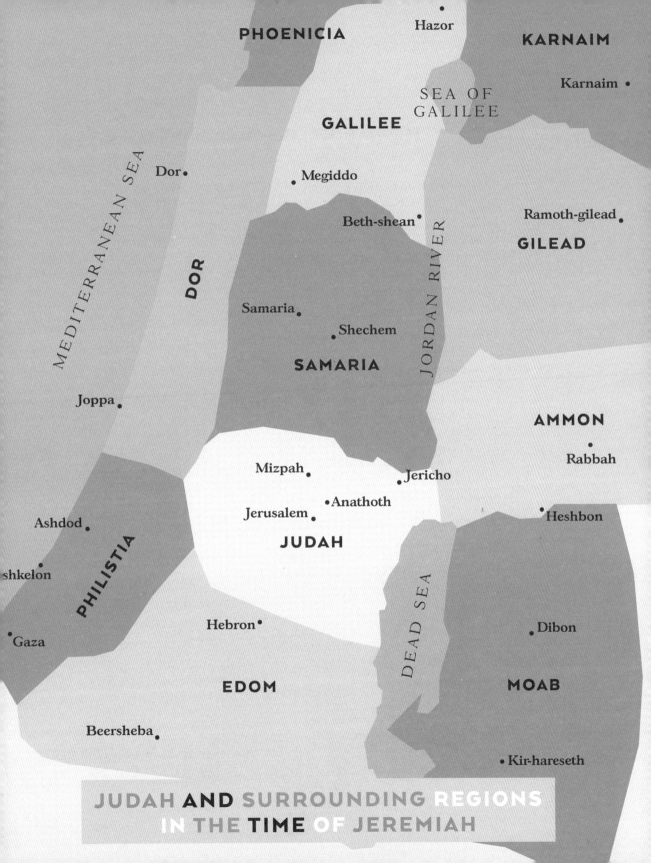

JUDAH **AND** SURROUNDING **REGIONS** **IN** THE **TIME** OF **JEREMIAH**

connect jeremiah

WITH THE REST OF SCRIPTURE

THE BOOK OF JEREMIAH MAKES CONNECTIONS TO BOTH THE OLD AND NEW TESTAMENT.

For example, Jeremiah has a lot of similarities to the book of Deuteronomy. In Deuteronomy God's people are preparing to enter the Promised Land. However, in Jeremiah the people of God will be exiled from the Promised Land. The book of Deuteronomy holds specific warnings to stay faithful to the Lord. Moses warns of the disastrous consequences that the Israelites would experience if they failed to do so. (Deuteronomy 28) Yet, Moses also leaves the Israelites with hope if the people would relent from their wicked ways and return to their Lord. Moses promises restoration for the repentant. (Deuteronomy 29-30)

Jeremiah picks up centuries after Moses, when the Israelites will face the consequences Moses warned them of. The failure to stay faithful breaks the covenant relationship with the Lord. But God was always working to restore this relationship throughout Scripture. In spite of the consequences, the Lord offers the hope of a future restoration — the same restoration promised in Deuteronomy. (Jeremiah 30-33)

MOSES	JEREMIAH
Warns the Israelites to stay faithful DEUTERONOMY 4:1-40	Urges Judah and Jerusalem to return to faithfulness JEREMIAH 4:1-4
Moses promises restoration for the repentant LEVITICUS 26:40-42	Jeremiah promises rescue for the exiled JEREMIAH 39:18
Moses leads the Israelites on a journey toward the Promised Land EXODUS 33:1	Jeremiah witnesses the Israelites' exile from the Promised Land JEREMIAH 29

The events that take place in Jeremiah set the stage for a long and challenging season for the Israelites. Living once again in captivity places them in a position to long for rescue. The heartbreak of Jeremiah as he witnesses the exile and enslavement of the Israelites points us forward to Jesus and into the New Testament. Just as Jeremiah was in deep sorrow over the condition of the Israelites enslaved by foreign powers, so Jesus was in deep sorrow over the condition of humanity enslaved by the powers of sin and death.

Take a moment and consider the specific connections between Jeremiah and Jesus:

1. They were both called/sent by God. (Jeremiah 1:4-5; John 17:3)
2. They served as the mouthpiece of God. (Jeremiah 1:6-10; Hebrews 1:1-2)
3. They were rejected by the people of God. (Jeremiah 1:19; Luke 4:28-29; 17:24-25)
4. They lived and witnessed the people of God under oppression from foreign enemies. (Jeremiah 52; Matthew 2:16-18; Mark 6:14-29)
5. They both watched as God's people vehemently rejected the message of God. (Jeremiah 43:1-7; John 12:36-37)

When we see these connections between Jesus and Jeremiah, take a moment to pause and reflect on the promise of hope that came centuries before Jesus came to earth. This promise was anticipated by the prophets of old and Jeremiah, the weeping prophet, helps us experience this anticipation ourselves as we await the return of the slain but risen King and sustainer of all creation.

Through it all, the character of God is on display, always remaining faithful even when His people are unfaithful. Allow Jeremiah to shape how you read the New Testament as you consider the situation the Israelites found themselves in — constantly at the mercy of foreign powers and waiting in eager anticipation for the promised rescue. This allows us to see Jesus clearly, not only throughout the pages of Jeremiah, but the entire Bible as the suffering servant who would bring final and complete rescue.

jeremiah 1

TODAY'S DATE:

Write a verse that summarizes the reading:

_____

_____

MAJOR MOMENT: God calls Jeremiah to prophesy to His people.

Jeremiah 1:1-3 gives us a very clear context of when and to whom Jeremiah was prophesying. Who are the three kings of Judah mentioned?

_____

_____

God came to Jeremiah with a specific message. What was His message? (Jeremiah 1:4-5) What was Jeremiah's first concern? (Jeremiah 1:6) How did God comfort Jeremiah? (Jeremiah 1:7-10)

_____

_____

Jeremiah was prophesying to a nation that had reverted to worshipping other gods and indulging in sin. (Jeremiah 1:16) Jeremiah 1:10 details Jeremiah's mission. What does it mean for Jeremiah "to pluck up and to break down" these practices? What do you think he was "to build and to plant" in their stead?

_____

_____

_____

God tells Jeremiah not to be dismayed or afraid of his work or the people he is confronting. (Jeremiah 1:8, 17) Why didn't Jeremiah need to be afraid? What was Jeremiah's responsibility from God? (Jeremiah 1:17) What was God's promise to Jeremiah? (Jeremiah 1:18-19) How does this encourage you to face your calling today?

_____

_____

_____

jeremiah 2

Write a verse that summarizes the reading:

_____

_____

MAJOR MOMENT: The Lord is faithful to an unfaithful Israel.

God reminds His people of their past faithfulness and of their special relationship with Him, (Jeremiah 2:1-3) and then asks them a very fair question: "What wrong did your fathers find in me?" (Jeremiah 2:4-5) This question highlights the futility of leaving God for "worthlessness." Why might they have pursued "worthlessness" after a relationship with God?

_____

_____

_____

What four types of leaders are specifically called out for leading the nation astray? (Jeremiah 2:8, 26) Why did the spiritual leaders (with shepherds referring to Israelite rulers) have a higher responsibility to God?

_____

_____

_____

What are the two evils that God outlines? (Jeremiah 2:13) What is the purpose of making a broken cistern (water tank) for yourself, when God is the fountain of living water?

_____

_____

_____

God desired to be reconciled to His people, and He had His prophets to prove it. He had called and disciplined His children, but they "devoured" the prophets. (Jeremiah 2:30) How does this relate to Jesus' sorrow over the same group of people? (Matthew 23:37)

_____

_____

_____

EXPERIENCE GUIDE · great and hidden things

jeremiah 3

Write a verse that summarizes the reading:

_____

_____

MAJOR MOMENT: God calls Israel to return to Him and promises healing.

Judah responds to God as if He has no reason to be angry (Jeremiah 3:4-5), and we may also start to wonder at the severity of God's words to them. This is why it is critical to understand the seriousness and longevity of Judah's sin and God's persistent mercy and pursuit of His people. What do you think about God's response to Judah's sin?

_____

_____

_____

Read Jeremiah 3:6-11. How are Israel and Judah contrasted? Why is Israel considered more righteous?

_____

_____

_____

What does God require of Israel? (Jeremiah 3:12-14) What does He require of us? (1 John 1:9)

_____

_____

_____

God makes it clear that the people only need to turn to Him, with a repentant heart and true desire for Him, and He will take care of the rest. (Jeremiah 3:10, 14-15, 22) This was the basis of God's relationship with Israel, and it is the basis of His relationship with us — His goodness and faithfulness. Is there anything in your life that you need to confess and turn from and return to God?

_____

_____

_____

jeremiah 4

Write a verse that summarizes the reading:

_____

_____

MAJOR MOMENT: Jeremiah warns of coming judgment by way of a Babylonian invasion and mourns for Israel.

God is concerned with the true repentance and permanent return of His people. (Jeremiah 4:1-2) What did God require of them as an indication of their return? What would God's response be to that return?

_____

_____

_____

The original Hebrew text suggests that Jeremiah 4:3 is addressed to individuals, rather than the people as a whole. They were challenged personally to break up the uncultivated ground of their spiritual lives and plant in good soil. What would it mean to invest in their spiritual lives? What does Jesus tell us about sowing among thorns? (Luke 8:14)

_____

_____

_____

Jeremiah sees he is speaking to an unrepentant nation, so he blows the trumpet of warning. (Jeremiah 4:5-8) God says the kings, officials, prophets and priests will be shocked and appalled. Of all people, why should these groups of people be the most prepared? What does this mean for us as God's "royal priesthood"? (1 Peter 2:5-9)

_____

_____

_____

Jeremiah 4:19-21 gives us a glimpse into why Jeremiah is referred to as "the weeping prophet." He is heartbroken over the fate of his people. When have you experienced this depth of emotion?

_____

_____

_____

jeremiah 5

Write a verse that summarizes the reading:

_____

_____

MAJOR MOMENT: Jeremiah searches for one righteous person in Jerusalem. God cannot tolerate Israel's injustice.

As He did with Sodom and Gomorrah (Genesis 18:22-33), God would pardon Jerusalem for the sake of the righteous, but it seems that no one righteous — following God's Word — can be found. (Jeremiah 5:1-5) What have the people of Jerusalem done to ignore the words of God? (Jeremiah 5:3; Zechariah 7:11-12)

_____

_____

_____

The Israelites show a false sense of security, no doubt one inspired by their false gods. How does Jeremiah 5:12-13 contrast with a healthy fear of the Lord?

_____

_____

_____

In Jeremiah 5:18 God says for the second time, "I will not make a full end of you" (Jeremiah 4:27). God has always promised to preserve a remnant of His people. (Isaiah 10:20-21; Micah 7:18-19; Romans 9:27-28; 11:5) How does this exemplify God's steadfast love and faithfulness to His people?

_____

_____

_____

God's character can be seen by the things He hates and cannot tolerate in His people. What are some of these things? (Jeremiah 5:25-29) What does this tell you about what God values and loves?

_____

_____

_____

week one notes

jeremiah 6

Write a verse that summarizes the reading:

_____

_____

MAJOR MOMENT: Jeremiah tells the Judeans to flee Jerusalem to escape the coming invasion.

Jeremiah calls for the Israelites to flee Jerusalem since an attack is impending. Jerusalem also seems to be the source of Israel's evil. (Jeremiah 6:7) As Jerusalem "keeps fresh her evil," it challenges us to examine what we "keep fresh." What are you nurturing or "keeping fresh" that keeps you from following faithfully after Jesus?

_____

_____

_____

_____

Read Jeremiah 6:13-15. Israel's priests and prophets are preaching that there is no need for concern, only "peace." This makes the people feel better for a little while, but it is no permanent healing because it is not true. Jeremiah has quite a different message from God, and while it was scary, it held healing and the potential for reconciliation. How can we discern whether we are being told what we want to hear or the truth of God's Word? What is the true source of peace? (Jeremiah 6:16; Matthew 11:29)

_____

_____

_____

As Israel was once an image of God's blessing in love to the nations, they would now be an example of God's discipline in love. (Jeremiah 6:18-19) What is the benefit of having the surrounding nations see God's justice in action?

_____

_____

_____

_____

jeremiah 7

Write a verse that summarizes the reading:

_____

_____

MAJOR MOMENT: Jeremiah gives a sermon at the temple.

Jeremiah 7 is known as Jeremiah's temple sermon, because God calls him to speak to the men worshipping there. The temple was the physical location of God's relationship with His people, so the people seem to believe that as long as the temple was there, God would be there. (Jeremiah 7:1-4) What they ignored was the temple was meant to be kept holy, along with those entering. (Jeremiah 7:5-15) What does God say He will do to the temple if His people do not repent?

_____

_____

How does this temple sermon connect with John 2:13-17?

_____

_____

The Israelites' offerings to God were part of many offerings to many gods. (Jeremiah 7:21-23) Not only that, but they did not include what God truly desired — obedience. (1 Samuel 15:22; Hosea 6:6) Why is obedience more valuable than a sacrificial gift? Have you ever tried to make a sacrificial gift to God in hopes that it makes up for another area of disobedience?

_____

_____

Perhaps it is no longer surprising to read that the Israelites did not "obey or incline their ear" (Jeremiah 7:24). What or who did they obey instead? (Jeremiah 7:24-26; 9:13-14) This is why "follow your heart" can be dangerous advice. What does it look like when you follow your heart when it is not in line with God's? What does it look like when you follow God's instruction? (Proverbs 3:1-8)

_____

_____

Jeremiah 7:30-31 gives us a glimpse of the horrors of Jerusalem at the time. How had God previously addressed this practice to the Israelites? (Leviticus 20:2-5)

_____

_____

jeremiah 8-9

TODAY'S DATE:

Write a verse that summarizes the reading:

MAJOR MOMENT: **Jeremiah 8:** Judgment is coming on Israel because of their faithlessness.
Jeremiah 9: God's goodness requires Him to punish evil.

Clearly the religious leaders were distorting God's Word and leading the Israelites astray. (Jeremiah 8:8-9) When listening to teaching or preaching, what clues tip you off to a twisting of God's Word?

Read Jeremiah 9:2. Jeremiah gets to the point where he wants to abandon his call. It has gotten too hard. When have you been tempted to abandon God's will? What hope does knowing Jeremiah had similar feelings give?

God, through Jeremiah, gives an outline of Israel's sin and then asks a simple question: "Shall I *not* punish them for these things?" (Jeremiah 9:3-9, emphasis added) While we know God is merciful and gracious, what kind of God would He be if He did not punish such injustice?

Jeremiah 9:23-24 gives such an incredible view into godly wisdom. In what things does a foolish person boast? Conversely, in what does a wise person boast? What a joy it is to know that we serve a God who delights in love, justice and righteousness!

jeremiah 10

Write a verse that summarizes the reading:

MAJOR MOMENT: Jeremiah contrasts false religion with the one true God.

How does Jeremiah 10:1-5 describe the gods and religions of the surrounding nations? How does that description contrast with the one true God? (Jeremiah 10:6-16)

Jeremiah 10:10 describes God as the "living" God. This is a characteristic we often see of God in Scripture. What does it mean to you that our God is living, active and engaged? (Hosea 1:10; 2 Corinthians 3:3)

Jeremiah takes on the personification of Jerusalem (or Zion) in Jeremiah 10:19-21. This is something we see him do in Lamentations as well. (Lamentations 2:20-22) Compare this cry of destruction from Zion in Jeremiah 10:19-21 with God's promise for restoration in Zion in Isaiah 54:1-3. What images do both passages use to illustrate Zion's state?

----

jeremiah 11

Write a verse that summarizes the reading:

_____

_____

MAJOR MOMENT: God reminds the Israelites of their covenant.

Jeremiah 11 opens with a reminder to the Jews about the covenant God made with their fathers through Moses after delivering them from Egyptian captivity. (Exodus 19-24; Jeremiah 11:1-8) This is a good opportunity for us to look back at the covenant God made with His people. What was the purpose of the covenant? (Exodus 19:4-6) What does this show about God's desires?

_____

_____

_____

_____

Jeremiah prophesied during the time of King Josiah, who had been given the Book of Law (which included the written covenant) after it had been lost for many years. What was the king's response to finding the Book of the Law? (2 Kings 22:8-13) Was this an appropriate response?

_____

_____

_____

_____

Jeremiah 11 was likely written after King Josiah's attempt at national reform, so we can assume it had been unsuccessful. Jeremiah 11:10 puts it plainly — they have broken the covenant. To obey God and maintain the covenant, the Israelites needed to keep God's Word always near them. (Joshua 1:8; Psalm 119:11) Although we are not bound to the Book of Law in the same way the Israelites were, what is the value in keeping God's Word in our hearts and minds?

_____

_____

_____

_____

week two notes

HOW THE NEW TESTAMENT
USES JEREMIAH

"But the LORD said to me, 'Do not say, "I am only a youth"; for to all to whom I send you, you shall go, and whatever I command you, you shall speak.'"
JEREMIAH 1:7

"Has this house, which is called by my name, become a den of robbers in your eyes? Behold, I myself have seen it, declares the LORD."
JEREMIAH 7:11

"But, O LORD of hosts, who judges righteously, who tests the heart and the mind, let me see your vengeance upon them, for to you have I committed my cause."
JEREMIAH 11:20

"I the LORD search the heart and test the mind, to give every man according to his ways, according to the fruit of his deeds."
JEREMIAH 17:10

"'Woe to the shepherds who destroy and scatter the sheep of my pasture!' declares the LORD. Therefore thus says the LORD, the God of Israel, concerning the shepherds who care for my people: 'You have scattered my flock and have driven them away, and you have not attended to them. Behold, I will attend to you for your evil deeds, declares the LORD.'"
JEREMIAH 23:1-2

"For I will satisfy the weary soul, and every languishing soul I will replenish."
JEREMIAH 31:25

"Behold, the days are coming, declares the LORD, when I will make a new covenant with the house of Israel and the house of Judah."
JEREMIAH 31:31

"I will make with them an everlasting covenant, that I will not turn away from doing good to them. And I will put the fear of me in their hearts, that they may not turn from me."
JEREMIAH 32:40

"Delivering you from your people and from the Gentiles—to whom I am sending you."
ACTS 26:17

"He said to them, 'It is written, "My house shall be called a house of prayer," but you make it a den of robbers.'"
MATTHEW 21:13

"And I will strike her children dead. And all the churches will know that I am he who searches mind and heart, and I will give to each of you according to your works."
REVELATION 2:23

"Behold, I am coming soon, bringing my recompense with me, to repay each one for what he has done."
REVELATION 22:12

"All who came before me are thieves and robbers, but the sheep did not listen to them."
JOHN 10:8

"Come to me, all who labor and are heavy laden, and I will give you rest."
MATTHEW 11:28

"For this is my blood of the covenant, which is poured out for many for the forgiveness of sins."
MATTHEW 26:28

"And likewise the cup after they had eaten, saying, 'This cup that is poured out for you is the new covenant in my blood.'"
LUKE 22:20

jeremiah 12

TODAY'S DATE:

Write a verse that summarizes the reading:

_____

_____

MAJOR MOMENT: Jeremiah laments his suffering and God mourns the loss of relationship with His people.

What is Jeremiah's complaint in Jeremiah 12:1-4? How does God respond to him in Jeremiah 12:5-6?

_____

_____

_____

Jeremiah is living a godly life in a godless world. How did Paul encourage the early Christians when they were facing a similar situation? (2 Timothy 3:10-13) What encouragement does Jesus give us in John 16:33? Does this influence the way you view persecution and suffering?

_____

_____

_____

Read Jeremiah 12:7-13. What loss is God mourning?

_____

_____

_____

The prophecies of judgment make Judah's situation seem unredeemable, but God never leaves His people in a hopeless place. What hope does He bring in Jeremiah 12:14-17?

_____

_____

_____

jeremiah 13

Write a verse that summarizes the reading:

_____

_____

MAJOR MOMENT: God illustrates His relationship with Judah through the ruined linen loincloth.

What does God instruct Jeremiah to do with his linen loincloth (a cloth tied around the waist, almost like a short skirt worn close to the body)? What is this meant to signify? (Jeremiah 13:1-11)

_____

_____

_____

The linen loincloth is closely associated with the priestly garments. (Leviticus 16:4; Ezekiel 44:17) In what ways is Judah like this loincloth — for better or worse? (Exodus 19:6; Jeremiah 13:8-11)

_____

_____

_____

What are the Judeans called to do? When should they do it? (Jeremiah 13:15-16)

_____

_____

_____

Jeremiah prophesies Judah's exile to Babylon (whom they had previously treated as allies), which we know would eventually happen. (Jeremiah 13:18-21; 2 Kings 24:1-12) Despite all of this, why was Judah still unable to do good? (Jeremiah 13:23; Psalm 16:2; John 15:4-5) How can we avoid the same cycle of sin and ignoring God's Word that Judah fell into?

_____

_____

_____

jeremiah 14

Write a verse that summarizes the reading:

_____

_____

MAJOR MOMENT: Jeremiah prophesies concerning the drought in Judah and Jeremiah attempts to intercede on their behalf.

Jeremiah 14 begins with God's words concerning a drought in Judah. After reading Deuteronomy 11:13-17 and the consequences of breaking the covenant with God, should this drought come as a surprise to God's people? Why or why not?

_____

_____

_____

_____

Many times Jeremiah is told by God not to pray for the people. (Jeremiah 7:16, 11:14, 14:11-12) Why might God have forbidden Jeremiah from praying on their behalf? (Exodus 32:10; Isaiah 1:13-15)

_____

_____

_____

_____

The people of Judah were taught by their priests to believe that because they were God's people He would keep anything bad from happening to them. (Jeremiah 14:13-16) So often we fall into this same thinking. While we aren't promised that nothing bad will happen to us, what are we promised? (Matthew 6:26; 11:28-30; John 4:14; 10:10, 28; 14:2-3; Ephesians 1:3; 2 Corinthians 1:3-4, 20; Romans 1:16-17; 1 Peter 1:3-5)

_____

_____

_____

_____

jeremiah 15

TODAY'S DATE:

Write a verse that summarizes the reading:

_____

_____

MAJOR MOMENT: God refuses to relent. Jeremiah laments his loneliness and God comforts him.

God prepares Jeremiah how to answer the question He knows will come from the people — "Where shall we go?" Essentially God says that whatever the people are for is where they will go. (Jeremiah 15:1-2) What are you living for? Where is it leading you?

_____

_____

_____

_____

Much of the judgment that is happening in Judah stems from the evil that King Manasseh set in motion decades previously. What does 2 Kings 21:1-9 tell us about Manasseh and what he did in Jerusalem?

_____

_____

_____

God has continually relented and spared His people, (Exodus 32:14; 1 Chronicles 21:15; Jeremiah 26:19) but at this point, He has wearied of mercy. (Jeremiah 15:5-9) What does God say He has done up to this point to keep from enacting judgment?

_____

_____

_____

Jeremiah brings his third complaint to God. (Jeremiah 15:10-18) He has been ostracized and abandoned because of his dedication to God's message. How does God respond to Jeremiah? (Jeremiah 15:19-21) Have you ever felt alone because of your belief in God and dedication to Him?

_____

_____

_____

jeremiah 16

Write a verse that summarizes the reading:

_____

_____

MAJOR MOMENT: God gives Jeremiah personal directives and promises His people will return to their land.

God gives Jeremiah specific rules relating to how he should live his life. What are they? Why are they given? (Jeremiah 16:1-4)

_____

_____

_____

What answer does God give for the time when Judah will ask what they have done wrong? (Jeremiah 16:10-13)

_____

_____

_____

God's judgment of Judah will come in the form of exile in Babylon, but what is the Israelites' final destination? (Jeremiah 16:13-15) What does this tell you about God's relationship with His people?

_____

_____

_____

_____

What is God revealing about Himself to His people? (Jeremiah 16:21) What is God revealing about Himself to you?

_____

_____

_____

_____

week three notes

jeremiah 17

Write a verse that summarizes the reading:

....

....

MAJOR MOMENT: God describes sin and its consequences and instructs Jeremiah to teach the Sabbath.

How is Judah's sin described in Jeremiah 17:1-3? What does this tell you about the nature of sin?

....

....

....

....

What differences describe an individual who trusts in man and an individual who trusts in God? (Jeremiah 17:5-8; Psalm 1:3) Why does a person who trusts in God need not fear in the face of crisis?

....

....

....

....

Read Jeremiah 17:19-27. What does God tell Jeremiah to tell Jerusalem concerning the Sabbath? Why does God command His people to have a day dedicated to rest in sanctuary with Him? (Genesis 2:2-3; Exodus 31:12-13; Deuteronomy 5:12-15; Isaiah 58:13-14) Is the Sabbath still important today? (Matthew 12:1-12; Mark 2:23-28)

....

....

....

....

jeremiah 18

Write a verse that summarizes the reading:

_____

_____

_____

MAJOR MOMENT: A potter works the clay vessel and Jeremiah seeks vengeance.

Read Jeremiah 18:1-11. Who is the potter representing? Who is the clay? What is the relationship like between the potter and the clay?

_____

_____

_____

_____

What do these scriptures suggest about the authority a creator has over his creation? What are God's rights over His creation? (Genesis 2:7; Isaiah 29:16; Romans 9:20-24; 2 Timothy 2:20-22)

_____

_____

_____

_____

What influence do the people of Judah have in how God shapes their future? (Jeremiah 18:7-11)

_____

_____

_____

Jeremiah's truth-telling was, perhaps unsurprisingly, not well received. (Jeremiah 18:18) Jeremiah's reaction to his enemies is different than what the Christian is called to do (Matthew 5:44; Romans 12:20) but what does it tell us about his passion and goals? (Jeremiah 18:19-23)

_____

_____

_____

jeremiah 19

Write a verse that summarizes the reading:

_____

_____

MAJOR MOMENT: Jeremiah speaks to the elders at the Valley of the Son of Himmon and renames it the Valley of Slaughter.

God calls Jeremiah to speak to the elders and priests in a very specific location. What is that location? Why is it significant that they gather there? (Jeremiah 7:31; 19:2-5) What is this place to be renamed? (Jeremiah 19:6)

_____

_____

_____

In Jeremiah 18, God spoke of clay yet to be fully formed, He is now using hardened clay as an example. How were the elders and the valley like the potter's earthenware flask? How is this different than the clay? (Jeremiah 19:10-15)

_____

_____

_____

_____

Jeremiah 19 speaks to the hardening, drying and stiffening that makes the vessel breakable and unmendable. Is there an area in your life where you have hardened to the point of breaking? What created this hardness? What can you do to soften?

_____

_____

_____

_____

_____

jeremiah 20

TODAY'S DATE:

Write a verse that summarizes the reading:

_____

_____

MAJOR MOMENT: Jeremiah is persecuted by Pashhur and laments his situation.

Remembering Jeremiah 19, what did Pashhur hear? Why was this threatening to him?

_____

_____

What was Pashhur's response to Jeremiah's prophecy? (Jeremiah 20:1-6) What would have been a godly response?

_____

_____

_____

Jeremiah 20:7-18 gives us a deep view into Jeremiah's psychological and spiritual state. What do you notice about his emotions? Can you identify with any of his experiences?

_____

_____

_____

Although Jeremiah is distraught, he cannot keep the Word of God shut up in himself. What does he compare it to? (Jeremiah 20:9)

_____

_____

_____

Jeremiah takes a sharp turn to remind himself (and us) of this truth about God: "But the LORD is with me as a dread warrior" (Jeremiah 20:11). How is the Lord like a warrior for the righteous?

_____

_____

jeremiah 21

Write a verse that summarizes the reading:

_____

_____

MAJOR MOMENT: God gives Jeremiah prophecies for the last kings of Judah.

Jeremiah 21 moves into Jeremiah's prophecies during the time of King Zedekiah. What is happening in Jerusalem that has King Zedekiah concerned? What is his hope? (Jeremiah 21:1-2)

_____

_____

_____

Read God's response in Jeremiah 21:3-7. Zedekiah was concerned about the immediate circumstances, but God speaks to immediate and future plans. What will God do immediately in the city? What will be the future outcome?

_____

_____

_____

What options has God set before His people? (Deuteronomy 30:15-20; Jeremiah 21:8-9) How does this relate to the options Jesus set out for us? (Matthew 7:13)

_____

_____

_____

God gives His people a way to survive, but they will still be captives for a time. God's justice could not be thwarted completely. (Jeremiah 21:11-12) Take some time to reflect on God's mercy in the midst of justice and write a prayer to Him.

_____

_____

_____

_____

week four notes

jeremiah 22

Write a verse that summarizes the reading:

_____

_____

MAJOR MOMENT: Jeremiah continues with prophecies for the sons of Josiah.

What charge does God give the king of Judah? (Jeremiah 22:1-3) Why does God care about justice? Why does God sometimes have the reputation of being unjust in our world?

_____

_____

_____

_____

God's words concerning Shallum (also known as Jehoahaz) and his brother Jehoiakim give us a clear view of what an unjust king looks like. For more information on Jehoahaz and Jahoiakim, read 2 Kings 23:30-24:7. What were some of the hallmarks of an unjust king? (Jeremiah 22:11-15, 17-18) Josiah, their father, was an example of a true and just king. What set him apart? (Jeremiah 22:15-16)

_____

_____

_____

_____

What is the evidence that King Josiah knew the Lord? (Jeremiah 22:16) Why does this evidence indicate knowledge of Him? (Deuteronomy 10:17-18)

_____

_____

_____

_____

jeremiah 23

Write a verse that summarizes the reading:

_____

_____

MAJOR MOMENT: Jeremiah tells of a coming Messiah and condemns the lying prophets.

Read Jeremiah 23:1-2. What were the shepherds doing to God's people? Who are these shepherds?

_____

_____

_____

Jeremiah 23 gives us a glimpse of the true and perfect Shepherd — Jesus, the righteous Branch of David. (Jeremiah 23:3-8) How is this Shepherd's care different than any other earthly shepherd? What does the life of the flock under the care of the true Shepherd look like?

_____

_____

_____

_____

Jeremiah continued his condemnation of false prophets who bring a message of false hope to the people. What is the core of their message? Why is this such a dangerous message? (Jeremiah 23:16-17)

_____

_____

_____

_____

These prophets were likely from the temple in Jerusalem — ideally the most holy and God-filled place. But that did not guarantee they were truly in relationship with God and telling His true Word. What was the only guarantee that the prophets would hear from God? (Jeremiah 23:22)

_____

_____

_____

BEHOLD, THE DAYS ARE COMING, DECLARES THE LORD, WHEN I WILL RAISE UP FOR DAVID A RIGHTEOUS BRANCH, AND HE SHALL REIGN AS KING AND DEAL WISELY, AND SHALL EXECUTE JUSTICE AND RIGHTEOUSNESS IN THE LAND. IN HIS DAYS JUDAH WILL BE SAVED, AND ISRAEL WILL DWELL SECURELY. AND THIS IS THE NAME BY WHICH HE WILL BE CALLED: "THE LORD IS OUR RIGHTEOUSNESS."

JEREMIAH 23:5-6

jeremiah 24

TODAY'S DATE:

Write a verse that summarizes the reading:

_____

_____

MAJOR MOMENT: Jeremiah has a vision about good and bad figs.

Jeremiah 24 consists of a vision that came to Jeremiah during a period of Babylonian exile around 597 B.C. (2 Kings 24:10-17)

Who did King Nebuchadnezzar take captive from Judah? (Jeremiah 24:1)

_____

_____

_____

Who does God equate with the good figs? (Jeremiah 24:4-7) Why are the captives regarded as good? What is God's plan for them? What did the captives do differently than those who stayed in Judah or fled to Egypt? (Jeremiah 21:8-10)

_____

_____

_____

Who does God equate with the bad figs? (Jeremiah 24:8-10) What is God's plan for them?

_____

_____

_____

God makes it clear to His people that a relationship with Him is not dependent on their physical location, religious rituals or national allegiance. What do you base your relationship with God on? When have you tried to base it on something else?

_____

_____

_____

jeremiah 25

Write a verse that summarizes the reading:

....

....

MAJOR MOMENT: Judah has refused to repent after many years of Jeremiah's prophecy. The nations around Judah will also drink the cup of God's wrath.

For how long has Jeremiah been prophesying to the people of Judah and Jerusalem? (Jeremiah 25:3) Has his message changed in all of these years? How have the people of Judah responded to his message? (Jeremiah 25:4-7)

....

....

....

What is God's plan for Judah? How will He utilize Babylon? (Jeremiah 25:8-14)

....

....

....

Once Judah has drunk the "cup of the Lord's wrath," who will drink it next? (Jeremiah 25:15-26) What is the purpose of their judgment?

....

....

....

Jeremiah's message to the nations in Jeremiah 25:15-38 was of God's wrath. What is our message to all nations? (Psalm 105:1; Matthew 10:7; 28:19-20; 2 Corinthians 5:14-21; Acts 2:37-40; 13:47; 1 Peter 3:15)

....

....

....

jeremiah 26

Write a verse that summarizes the reading:

_____

_____

MAJOR MOMENT: Jeremiah brings every word of God's message despite threats of death.

God commands Jeremiah to speak every word He is going to tell him — it's all or nothing. (Jeremiah 26:2) We can encounter a similar danger when we take parts of God's Word out of context and don't strive to understand God in His entirety. What is the danger of only listening to or obeying some of God's Word?

_____

_____

_____

God tells His people if they don't listen to Him, He will make them like Shiloh — the city that originally housed His tabernacle. (Joshua 18:1) As a reminder, what happened at Shiloh? Although we don't know exactly when or how it was completely destroyed, what does Scripture suggest that it means to be made "like Shiloh"? (Psalm 78:60-66; 1 Samuel 4:3-11; Jeremiah 7:12-15; 26:3-6)

_____

_____

_____

Based on what we have learned about the majority of priests and prophets at the time, how was Jeremiah's message different than their typical message? (Jeremiah 23:16-17; 26:7-13)

_____

_____

_____

Jeremiah has been persistent and faithful to his God-given calling despite great opposition and seeing very little fruit of his labors. (Jeremiah 26:14-15) What in your life is requiring persistence and faithfulness? What keeps you moving forward?

_____

_____

_____

week five notes

jeremiah 27

Write a verse that summarizes the reading:

....

....

MAJOR MOMENT: God gives temporary power to Nebuchadnezzar and calls His people to submit.

What does God want to establish about Himself before moving into the details of His prophecy? (Jeremiah 27:5) Is this an important reminder for you today?

....

....

....

....

What physical representation did God command Jeremiah to have when giving his message? How did it correlate with what Jeremiah was saying? (Jeremiah 27:2, 6-15)

....

....

....

....

What were the priests prophesying about the vessels of the Lord's house? (Jeremiah 27:16-17) What had happened to these important temple objects? (2 Kings 24:10-17; Daniel 1:1-2) What does God say about the vessels that were taken and those that still remained in His temple? (Jeremiah 27:18-22)

....

....

....

....

jeremiah 28

Write a verse that summarizes the reading:

_____

_____

MAJOR MOMENT: Hananiah offers an opposing prophecy and dies as a result.

Hananiah also had a prophecy concerning the temple vessels. What was his message? (Jeremiah 28:1-4) What did he do to physically represent his message? (Jeremiah 28:10-11)

_____

_____

_____

Jeremiah acknowledges that Hananiah's prophecy is more pleasant than his — even praying it comes true! (Jeremiah 28:5-6) The problem is that it's a lie. What past and future evidence does Jeremiah give that he is telling the truth and Hananiah is lying? (Jeremiah 28:8-9)

_____

_____

_____

This interaction between Jeremiah and Hananiah gives us insight into the conflict and opposition that Jeremiah was facing as a true prophet of God. It must have also been confusing for those who were witnessing their opposing prophecies. Have you been in a situation where you witnessed two opposite teachings about God? How did you know who or what to trust?

_____

_____

_____

_____

Hananiah's punishment for making God's people trust in a lie was severe: death. (Jeremiah 28:15-17) Why is misleading people such a serious sin? What does it say about God's character?

_____

_____

_____

jeremiah 29

Write a verse that summarizes the reading:

_____

_____

MAJOR MOMENT: God sends a message of encouragement to the exiles and a message of judgment to those who refused Babylon's yoke.

Who does Jeremiah 29:1 say this letter is to? What is God's message for these people? (Jeremiah 29:5-9) Why might He encourage them to settle in and live life as normally as possible?

_____

_____

_____

God's message through Jeremiah has been consistent. They can expect to be in exile for 70 years. (Jeremiah 25:12; 29:10; Daniel 9:2) What is God's plan and Judah's hope at the end of the 70-year exile? (Jeremiah 29:10-15)

_____

_____

_____

This chapter holds arguably one of the best known verses in all of Scripture — Jeremiah 29:11. Have you heard this verse before? Does reading in context of the story of Judah change your interpretation of it?

_____

_____

_____

Read Jeremiah 29:15-19. This is God's message about the people who stayed in Jerusalem. These people not only ignored His call to righteousness but also would not submit to God's judgment through exile. Would they be able to evade judgment forever? What can we learn through them about submitting to correction the first time?

_____

_____

_____

jeremiah 30

Write a verse that summarizes the reading:

_____

_____

MAJOR MOMENT: Judah and Israel will be restored to God and their land.

Jeremiah spent most of his life prophesying to the kingdom of Judah, but this time God sends a message for Judah and Israel — His original united nation torn apart because of King Solomon's idolatry. (1 Kings 11) What is the core of the message God wants Jeremiah to record for His people? (Jeremiah 30:1-3)

_____

_____

God reminds His people He will bring restoration and unity back to them. His use of the name Jacob — the man whose name God changed to Israel and the father of the 12 tribes — reminds them that He has not forgotten His promise. (Jeremiah 30:7, 10) What is the summary of God's covenant promise to His people? (Jeremiah 30:8-9)

_____

_____

David has been long dead and no direct descendant of his has sat on the throne in many years. So, what does God mean in verse 9 when He says, "But they shall serve the LORD their God and David their king, whom I will raise up for them"? (Ezekiel 34:23-24; Hosea 3:5; Luke 1:31-33)

_____

_____

Jesus was the plan from the beginning. Jeremiah, as well as many other Old Testament books and prophets, give us an incredible view of God's plan unfolding. God would have to discipline His children, but His plan is eternal restoration. (Jeremiah 30:11, 21-24) Does this give you hope for the future? Why or why not?

_____

_____

Jeremiah 30:24 gives us an interesting perspective. God knew that the people (including us) would not be able to fully understand His words and intentions until the "latter days." Take heart that all that God has planned is not yet done and praise Him for what He has done so far in the person of Jesus Christ. Write a brief prayer of thanksgiving and praise.

_____

jeremiah 31

Write a verse that summarizes the reading:

_____

_____

MAJOR MOMENT: A new and better covenant is promised.

Read Jeremiah 31:1-3. God reminds His people that throughout their relationship, just because they suffered or He seemed far away, did not mean that His favor or love was any less present. (Romans 11:29) What does God's everlasting love and faithfulness look like in your life?

_____

_____

_____

_____

What blessings can be expected after restoration? (Jeremiah 31:12-14) What transformation will God offer for His people? (Jeremiah 31:13)

_____

_____

_____

_____

God doesn't just give hope for a restoration of the old covenant; He promises a new and better covenant. How is the new covenant different than the old covenant? How is it the same? (Jeremiah 31:31-34; Ezekiel 36:26-28; Luke 22:20; Romans 11:26-29; Hebrews 8:6-13; 9:11-10:1; 2 Corinthians 3:4-11)

_____

_____

_____

_____

week six notes

jeremiah 32

Write a verse that summarizes the reading:

_____

_____

MAJOR MOMENT: God instructs Jeremiah to purchase a field as a sign of promised future restoration.

Who imprisoned Jeremiah? What was Jeremiah's supposed crime? (Jeremiah 32:1-5)

_____

_____

_____

Jeremiah doesn't respond directly to the king's questions. Instead, he offers Zedekiah a sign that God gave him. What had God commanded Jeremiah to do? What was the bigger message God was communicating? (Jeremiah 32:6-15)

_____

_____

_____

Jeremiah takes time to recount God's relationship with His people — from creation to their current situation — and it seems as if Jeremiah doesn't quite understand what his purchase of a field has to do with this big picture. (Jeremiah 32:16-25) What reassurance does God give Jeremiah after recounting this story? (Jeremiah 32:27) Does this truth bring reassurance to you?

_____

_____

_____

Although God was temporarily giving His land away, (Jeremiah 32:25-28) He prepared His people to return and always promised a future restoration, because our God "rejoices in doing them good" (Jeremiah 32:36-41). What good have you seen God do?

_____

_____

_____

great and hidden things • EXPERIENCE GUIDE

jeremiah 33

Write a verse that summarizes the reading:

_____

_____

MAJOR MOMENT: The Lord promises His people peace and prosperity and that His covenant can never be broken.

Despite the fact that Jeremiah is still imprisoned, God continued to speak to him and use him. Jeremiah is called the "weeping prophet," but God gives him a message of great joy and hope. What does God promise to bring to the city of Jerusalem and the people of Israel and Judah? (Jeremiah 33:1-8)

_____

_____

_____

Read Jeremiah 33:9. Where Jerusalem was once a warning for the surrounding nations, (Jeremiah 24:9) they will become an image of God's glory through His goodness and prosperity. What will this display of God's glory cause the "nations of the earth" to do? How are we also a display of God's glory? (Romans 8:29; 2 Corinthians 3:18; Colossians 3:9-17)

_____

_____

_____

Jeremiah 33:14-26 gives us a view of God's future plans for His covenant with Israel and the house of Judah. What key characteristic is God making clear about His covenant? (Jeremiah 33:20-21, 25-26)

_____

_____

_____

We looked at the branch promised to King David in Jeremiah 23, but Jeremiah 33 also references a promise God made with the Levitical priests. (Jeremiah 33:17-22) How does Jesus fulfill both God's promise of an eternal king and priest? (Matthew 2:2; 27:11; 1 Timothy 2:5; Hebrews 6:20; Revelation 19:14)

_____

_____

_____

jeremiah 34

Write a verse that summarizes the reading:

_____

_____

MAJOR MOMENT: Jeremiah prophesies about Zedekiah's future and against Judah's treatment of slaves.

Jeremiah 34-39 tell the stories of Judah's failing leadership. They are not chronological but grouped together to highlight Jeremiah's interactions and God's dealings with ungodly kings.

Jeremiah 34 tells of two prophecies from Jeremiah. What is the first and who is it for? (Jeremiah 34:1-7)

_____

_____

_____

_____

What has just happened when Jeremiah gives his second prophecy of the chapter? (Jeremiah 34:8-11) What does God's law say concerning Hebrew slaves? (Deuteronomy 15:12-18)

_____

_____

_____

_____

King Zedekiah attempts to honor a part of God's law, but he and the people revert back to their old way. (Jeremiah 34:12-16) What is the result of their partial obedience? (Jeremiah 34:17-22) When have you obeyed God but turned back when obedience got too hard, costly or inconvenient? What was the outcome?

_____

_____

_____

_____

jeremiah 35

Write a verse that summarizes the reading:

_____

_____

MAJOR MOMENT: The Rechabites exemplify obedience.

The story in Jeremiah 35 is not chronologically after Jeremiah 34, but it serves as a contrast to the partial obedience of Judah. What commands from their forefather Jonadab were they obedient to? (Jeremiah 35:6-10)

_____

_____

God doesn't offer moral judgment on the specific commands the Rechabites followed, but He does commend the absolute obedience to their father for over 200 years.[1] (Jeremiah 35:12-14) What was the Rechabites' reward for their obedience?

_____

_____

Why is obedience to God important to our faith? (John 15:9-14; 1 Peter 1:14-19; 2:12; 1 John 2:1-6) How do we know whether we are being obedient or not? (Romans 2:13-15; 1 John 5:2-3; 2 John 1:5-6)

_____

_____

Obedience is not something that comes naturally to most people. It can feel dangerous, but obedience to God is the safest, surest option. How can we know that obedience to God is safe? (Psalm 119:1-6; Luke 11:28; 2 Corinthians 3:17; Romans 2:7-10)

_____

_____

Friend, if you've lacked obedience in the past, fear not! It's never too late to begin following God and practicing obedience. Take some time to write a prayer of praise for God's grace and mercy to forgive our sins. (Hebrews 10:16-18)

_____

_____

[1] Dockery, D. S., Butler, T. C., Church, C. L., Scott, L. L., Ellis Smith, M. A., White, J. E., & Holman Bible Publishers (Nashville, T.. (1992). *Holman Bible Handbook* (pp. 421–423). Nashville, TN: Holman Bible Publishers.

jeremiah 36

Write a verse that summarizes the reading:

_____

_____

MAJOR MOMENT: God commands Jeremiah to write a scroll of all of Jeremiah's prophecies to give to Jehoiakim.

What reason does God give Jeremiah for writing the scroll of prophecies? (Jeremiah 36:1-3)

_____

_____

_____

Baruch reads the scroll of Jeremiah's prophecies many times to many people on this feast day, but we see two distinct reactions. How did the scribes and officials respond? (Jeremiah 36:11-19) How did King Jehoiakim and his servants respond? (Jeremiah 36:20-26)

_____

_____

_____

What do you think Jehoiakim was hoping would happen by getting rid of God's Word? What did happen instead? (Jeremiah 36:27-32)

_____

_____

_____

We may be tempted to act similarly by ignoring or rejecting parts of God's Word that seem too difficult or hard to understand. However, we know that God's Word is eternal and unchanging, despite all of the changes around us. Are there any parts of God's Word that you are tempted to ignore or reject? Why or why not?

_____

_____

_____

week seven notes

HEBREW WORD STUDY: SHUV

The Hebrew word **Shuv** is used throughout the Old Testament to describe someone turning away from or toward something. It is often used in relationship to God's chosen people who find themselves in a repetitive history of turning away from God and toward worthless idols. It is also used in the midst of their persecution, when they turn back to God in anticipation of rescue. Jeremiah uses this Hebrew word more often than any other Old Testament writer. His usage of **Shuv** can be broken down into five primary categories:

CATEGORIES OF USAGE:

Calls for Judah to repent and turn back to God.
There is a sense of covenant renewal and loyalty to the Lord.

JEREMIAH 3:12; 4:1

Call for Judah to turn away from wickedness and evil.
This includes repentance.

JEREMIAH 18:11

Description of Judah and Israel and their backsliding ways.

JEREMIAH 3:19; 11:10

Description of the Lord turning to Judah with judgement.

JEREMIAH 4:28; 21:4

Description of Israel's repentance and restoration.

JEREMIAH 31:18-19

If we are God's people, then we must turn away from evil and return to the Lord. Jeremiah's message is an echo of Elijah's in 1 Kings 18:21. Worshipping the One True God and worshipping idols are paths that lead in opposite directions.

ENGLISH DEFINITION:

To turn/return

5 CATEGORIES OF USAGE

שׁוּב

JEREMIAH 8:4 USES A PLAY ON WORDS.

The verb "turn" has a double direction (toward or away) and can be physical or spiritual in nature

turn   return

COVENANT

faithlessness   faithfulness

WORD USAGE

Occurs over 1,000 times in the Old Testament

Jeremiah uses it more than any other Old Testament writer (about 109 times)

10% of the total word usage is in Jeremiah

jeremiah 37

Write a verse that summarizes the reading:

_____

_____

MAJOR MOMENT: Zedekiah questions Jeremiah in prison.

King Zedekiah asks Jeremiah to intercede on Jerusalem's behalf and inquire about the Babylonian siege. What has happened that might make Zedekiah feel hopeful the Babylonians were permanently gone? (Jeremiah 37:5) What does God tell Jeremiah to say to Zedekiah? (Jeremiah 37:6-10)

_____

_____

_____

Why is Jeremiah imprisoned? (Jeremiah 37:11-15) What evidence is there that Jeremiah is a traitor? (Jeremiah 27) Are the charges true?

_____

_____

_____

Zedekiah secretly comes to Jeremiah, likely in hopes of a different message from God. Has God's message changed? (Jeremiah 21:7; 37:16-17)

_____

_____

_____

Jeremiah has been faithful to bring a difficult message to people who are unresponsive. He hasn't backed down or changed any of God's words. He has been steadfast and faithful. Who have you seen live a similarly steadfast life? What brought them strength in the midst of adversity?

_____

_____

_____

jeremiah 38

Write a verse that summarizes the reading:

_____

_____

MAJOR MOMENT: Jeremiah is saved from the cistern and is visited by Zedekiah.

Jeremiah is held again for the same reason: his prophecy that Babylon would conquer Jerusalem and the people should surrender. Where did the officials take Jeremiah instead of a prison? (Jeremiah 38:1-6)

_____

_____

_____

Who saved Jeremiah from death? (Jeremiah 38:7-13) How is this similar to the parable of the Good Samaritan? (Luke 10:25-37)

_____

_____

_____

King Zedekiah was constantly being swayed in different directions by the people around him. (Jeremiah 38:4) He was also afraid of man's judgment. (Jeremiah 38:19) He was clearly interested in what Jeremiah said and met with him in secret multiple times. Ultimately Zedekiah was influenced more by his officials than Jeremiah. (Jeremiah 38:5, 24-26) What wisdom does Proverbs 29:25 give us about situations like these?

_____

_____

_____

What can we learn from the difference in Jeremiah's and Zedekiah's response to outward pressure?

_____

_____

_____

jeremiah 39

Write a verse that summarizes the reading:

_____

_____

MAJOR MOMENT: Jerusalem is conquered, Zedekiah is punished for his faithlessness and Ebed-melech is rewarded for his faithfulness.

After all the wisdom and consistent words from God that Jeremiah gave to Zedekiah, Zedekiah still ran in fear when Jerusalem fell. (Jeremiah 39:4) What happened to Zedekiah and the people of Jerusalem because they didn't trust God's promise to deliver them if they surrendered? (Jeremiah 39:4-10)

_____

_____

_____

_____

Ebed-melech demonstrated his faith in God by standing up to the king and saving Jeremiah. (Jeremiah 38:7-13; 39:15-18) What was he promised because of his trust in God? What are we promised because of our trust in God? (Isaiah 26:3; Psalm 25:10; Romans 8:28; Ephesians 2:4-10; 1 Peter 1:3-5)

_____

_____

_____

_____

What can you learn about trusting God in the midst of incredibly difficult circumstances from Jeremiah and Ebed-melech?

_____

_____

_____

_____

jeremiah 40

Write a verse that summarizes the reading:

_____

_____

MAJOR MOMENT: Jeremiah is released and stays in Judah under Gedaliah.

After Jerusalem was taken by Babylon, Jeremiah is rounded up with the rest of the captives. Nebuzaradan obviously realized Jeremiah was not meant to be bound with the rest of the Judeans and let him go. (Jeremiah 39:11-12; 40:1-4) Unlike the people of Judah, the Babylonians were able to see the truth of Jeremiah's prophecies and gave him respect. How is Jeremiah's experience similar to Jesus' experience in Matthew 13:53-58?

_____

_____

_____

_____

Because of Jeremiah's standing with the Babylonians, they gave him the choice to go wherever he wanted. Where did Jeremiah choose to go? (Jeremiah 40:5-6)

_____

_____

_____

Who was left in Judah at this time? (2 Kings 25:12; Jeremiah 39:10; 40:7) Who was positioned as their governor? And what was his message to his fellow Judeans? (2 Kings 25:22-24; Jeremiah 40:7-12) Was this in agreement with what Jeremiah had proclaimed to the exiles and the remnant? (Jeremiah 25:11; 29:1-10)

_____

_____

_____

_____

What warning does Johanan give Gedaliah? (Jeremiah 40:13-15)

_____

_____

jeremiah 41

Write a verse that summarizes the reading:

_____

_____

MAJOR MOMENT: Ishmael murders Gedaliah and attempts to take the remnant to the Ammonites until Johanan intervenes.

Despite sincere attempts at rebuilding a life under Babylonian rule for the remnant in Judah, Gedaliah was killed by Ishmael, a member of David's royal house and likely the highest ranking man in Judah. (Jeremiah 41:1-3) Who else was killed in this attack?

_____

_____

_____

Ishmael's second attack occurs the next day on 80 men who were coming from Israel to worship at the temple. (Jeremiah 41:4-8) Why did Ishmael save 10 of these men?

_____

_____

_____

While we don't know his exact motive, we know that Ishmael decided to act in his own strength rather than wait patiently for God. When are you most tempted to act in your own strength rather than wait on God?

_____

_____

_____

Johanan rescued the people from Ishmael as they were on their way to the Ammonites. Where does Johanan plan to take them instead? What is his reasoning? (Jeremiah 41:11-18)

_____

_____

_____

great and hidden things · EXPERIENCE GUIDE

week eight notes

jeremiah 42-43

Write a verse that summarizes the reading:

_____

_____

MAJOR MOMENT: Jeremiah 42: God commands the remnant to stay in Judah where He will bless them. **Jeremiah 43**: Johanan and the remnant flee to Egypt to seek safety.

Before leaving for Egypt, Johanan asks Jeremiah for mercy and direction from God. (Jeremiah 42:1-3) What does Johanan promise to do in response to whatever God asks? (Jeremiah 42:5-6)

_____

_____

_____

God, through Jeremiah, repeats what He has said before, "Do not go to Egypt" (Jeremiah 42:7-17). What does God promise those who trust His provision and stay in His land?

_____

_____

_____

What is promised for those who decide to go to Egypt? (Jeremiah 42:13-22) Why were God's people tempted to go to Egypt? What did they think they would find there? (Isaiah 31:1)

_____

_____

_____

Despite Johanan's promises to do whatever God commanded, he did none of it. (Jeremiah 43:4-7) He seemed to know that obedience to God would bring wellness, (Jeremiah 42:6) and yet still couldn't trust in God's command because it seemed so counterintuitive. Have you had to trust God's wisdom when it seemed contrary to human wisdom? How did you know it was godly wisdom? What was the result?

_____

_____

_____

great and hidden things · EXPERIENCE GUIDE

66

jeremiah 44

Write a verse that summarizes the reading:

_____

_____

MAJOR MOMENT: The remnant in Egypt turn to idolatry.

Read Jeremiah 44:1-6. Who is Jeremiah speaking to? What had they witnessed in Jerusalem and all of Judah? What should this have taught them?

_____

_____

_____

What "great evil" did the remnant in Egypt commit? (Jeremiah 44:7-8) How is this also an evil act against themselves?

_____

_____

_____

The remnant in Egypt attributed all of their prosperity to their new, false gods and their times of distress to the One True God. (Jeremiah 44:15-19) In reality, it was the exact opposite. How does Jeremiah explain what was really happening? (Ecclesiastes 8:11-12; Jeremiah 44:20-23)

_____

_____

_____

Why is it foolish, and potentially dangerous, to always ascribe earthly prosperity to God's pleasure? (Psalm 92:7; 97:28; Proverbs 37:7-11, 16; Jeremiah 12:1)

_____

_____

_____

PAGAN GODS
IN THE OLD TESTAMENT

Pagan god	Worshipped in	Biblical reference
AMON	EGYPT	JEREMIAH 46:25; NAHUM 3:8
ASHTORETH	ASSYRIA	JEREMIAH 7:18; 1 KINGS 11:33
BAAL	CANAAN	JEREMIAH 2:8; 7:9; 19:5; JUDGES 2:11
BEL/MARDUK	BABYLON	JEREMIAH 50:2; 51:44
CHEMOSH	MOAB	JEREMIAH 48:7, 13, 46
MILCOM	AMMON	JEREMIAH 49:1, 3
MOLECH	AMMON	JEREMIAH 32:35

jeremiah 45

Write a verse that summarizes the reading:

_____

_____

MAJOR MOMENT: Jeremiah gives Baruch a message.

Who is Jeremiah's message for in Jeremiah 45? What is his job? (Jeremiah 45:1)

_____

_____

_____

What was Baruch's response to all that was happening in Judah? (Jeremiah 45:3)

_____

_____

_____

Although Jeremiah 45 is much later in the book, it took place chronologically after the events of Jeremiah 36:1-12. What had just taken place to leave Baruch so despondent?

_____

_____

_____

How does God show He understands Baruch's pain? (Jeremiah 45:4) What promise does God give Baruch to comfort him through the rest of the judgment that will still come? (Jeremiah 45:5)

_____

_____

_____

jeremiah 46

Write a verse that summarizes the reading:

_____

_____

MAJOR MOMENT: God promises judgment on Egypt.

The following few chapters are God's pronounced judgments on foreign nations who oppressed His people. What nation is Jeremiah 46 addressed to? What specific wrongdoing is mentioned? (2 Kings 23:29; 2 Chronicles 35:20-24; Jeremiah 46:1-2)

_____

_____

_____

The Day of the Lord is a term we see often in Scripture and is used in Jeremiah 46:10 to reference God's judgment of Egypt. The Day of the Lord is generally used in reference to God's judgment, but also holds a promise for those who have trusted in God. What does 1 Thessalonians 5:1-10 say about the final Day of the Lord?

_____

_____

_____

What was one way God would bring judgment on Egypt? (Jeremiah 46:13, 26)

_____

_____

Read another prophecy concerning Egypt in Ezekiel 29:12-16. How would Egypt serve as a reminder to God's people?

_____

_____

What promise of restoration does God give the Egyptians? (Jeremiah 46:26) What promise does God give His people at the end of this prophecy? (Jeremiah 46:27-28)

_____

_____

jeremiah 47

TODAY'S DATE:

Write a verse that summarizes the reading:

_____

_____

MAJOR MOMENT: God promises judgment on the Philistines.

What is the next group of people that will be punished? (Jeremiah 47:1)

_____

_____

_____

Read Jeremiah 47:5-7. While Jeremiah is aware that Philistia brought judgment on themselves, he still wishes God's sword would be put down. What does God use His sword to do? (Deuteronomy 32:41; Ezekiel 21:3-5)

_____

_____

_____

_____

_____

What is the charge that God's sword was given? (Jeremiah 47:4, 7) When do you think the sword will be able to be "quiet" and sheathed again?

_____

_____

_____

_____

_____

week nine notes

jeremiah 48

TODAY'S DATE:

Write a verse that summarizes the reading:

_____

_____

MAJOR MOMENT: God promises judgment on Moab.

Moab was close to Judah, and although they experienced times of peace, they were generally considered an enemy of God's people.

What is one of Moab's defining characteristics that we see in this chapter? (Jeremiah 28:7, 11-14, 17-18, 29-30) What is the only source of true trust and pride? (Jeremiah 9:24; 1 Corinthians 1:28-31)

_____

_____

_____

Read Jeremiah 48:13. What was Chemosh? (1 Kings 11:7, 33) How was this related to what happened in Bethel? (1 Kings 12:27-30)

_____

_____

_____

This oracle also ends with a promise of restoration. (Jeremiah 48:47) What does this tell you about the character of God?

_____

_____

_____

This chapter is full of vivid imagery of what would happen to Moab. What imagery stands out to you the most?

_____

_____

_____

jeremiah 49

Write a verse that summarizes the reading:

_____

_____

MAJOR MOMENT: God promises judgment on Ammon, Edom, Damascus, Kedar, Hadzor and Elam.

Jeremiah 49 addresses many different regions surrounding Judah. What reasons are given for these regions' judgment?

Ammon	Edom	Damascus (Capital city of Syria)	Kedar and Hadzor	Elam
Jeremiah 49:1, 4	*Jeremiah 49:16; Joel 3:19; Ezekiel 25:12-14*	*Jeremiah 49:25-26; 1 Kings 20*	*Jeremiah 49:31*	*Jeremiah 49:35; Ezekiel 32:24*

Some of the reasoning may not seem obvious. What was the problem with Kedar and Hadzor living at "ease" and dwelling "secure"? How do you imagine they obtained their ease and security?

_____

_____

Some of the regions in this chapter are also promised restoration. We don't know exactly how or when that happens, but we do see many of these regions experiencing revival through the Holy Spirit, brought by Jesus' sacrifice. What regions are present at the early church Pentecost? (Acts 2:1-10)

_____

_____

jeremiah 50

TODAY'S DATE:

Write a verse that summarizes the reading:

_____

_____

MAJOR MOMENT: God promises judgment on Babylon.

God's prophecy for Babylon is the longest and most intense of the series. During Babylon's time of judgment, what will the exiles from Israel and Judah be doing? (Jeremiah 50:4-5)

_____

_____

_____

How did the enemies of God's people excuse their own evil? (Jeremiah 50:7) Is this a reasonable excuse? Why or why not?

_____

_____

_____

Throughout Jeremiah we have seen that Babylon, and specifically Nebuchadnezzar, was used by God in His sovereignty as a tool of discipline for His people, but that did not excuse them from the evil they had done. (Jeremiah 50:17-18) How did King Nebuchadnezzar describe his experience with God's sovereignty at the end of his life? (Daniel 4:34-37)

_____

_____

_____

What is God's plan for Israel? (Jeremiah 50:19-20) How does God describe His relationship to His people now? (Jeremiah 50:33-34)

_____

_____

_____

EXPERIENCE GUIDE • great and hidden things

75

jeremiah 51

Write a verse that summarizes the reading:

_____

_____

MAJOR MOMENT: Jeremiah's prophecy of judgment is brought to Babylon.

Israel and Judah often cried out that they had been forsaken by God. Why might they have thought they were forsaken? What was the reality? (Jeremiah 51:5)

_____

_____

_____

Read Jeremiah 51:15-19. How is God different from the gods of the Babylonians?

_____

_____

_____

While we likely don't have golden gods, we do have pervasive idols in our lives. Is there anything in your life that you cling to instead of the sovereign God? What comfort, if any, does it bring?

_____

_____

_____

What kind of tool is Babylon likened to? (Jeremiah 51:20-23)

_____

_____

After finishing his prophecy, what does Jeremiah tell Seraiah to do? (Jeremiah 51:59-64) What did this communicate about the permanence of Babylon's fate?

_____

_____

_____

jeremiah 52

Write a verse that summarizes the reading:

_____

_____

MAJOR MOMENT: The fall of Jerusalem is retold.

Jeremiah 52 is an appendix to Jeremiah's prophecies, likely not written by Jeremiah, but borrowed almost exactly from 2 Kings 24:18-25:30. Not only is this chapter recounted in 2 Kings, but we have heard parts of it earlier in Jeremiah. (Jeremiah 39-40) What is the purpose of recounting it here at the end of Jeremiah's prophecies?

_____

_____

God revealed a lot of His plan, character and sovereignty to Jeremiah. Jeremiah 52 serves as a testament to the truth of those revelations. After reading this book, what have you learned about Jeremiah's relationship with God? How is it similar to your relationship with God? How is it different?

_____

_____

_____

Read Hebrews 11. How did Jeremiah exhibit this true faith? What was Jeremiah looking forward to? (Jeremiah 31:31-34) What has been revealed to us even more clearly about the new covenant? (Hebrews 8:6-13; 9:11-15)

_____

_____

_____

After reflecting on the book of Jeremiah, take some time to write a prayer of praise for God's goodness in His sovereignty.

_____

_____

_____

week ten notes

extra notes

extra notes

extra notes

What have you learned about God through the study of Jeremiah?

REFLECT ON
jeremiah

As we wrap up our study, take a moment to consider the prophet Jeremiah and the situation he found himself in as a weeping and suffering prophet. Jeremiah was fully committed to doing the work of the Lord. Sadly, his commitment and faithfulness were met with persecution from his own people, resulting in tremendous sorrow and pain.

This example is often true for us today. As believers, we are also given a particular task. We are called to be ambassadors of Christ. (2 Corinthians 5) As ambassadors, we reflect Christ to a broken and hurting world. We may also be met with persecution and pain. The extent and severity will vary, but regardless we all have a decision to make. Will we stay faithful in the face of opposition like Jeremiah? Will we walk out our calling with confidence and rely on the Lord to speak through us?

Throughout our study of the book of Jeremiah, we saw the tragedy of exile as a consequence of sin. Today, we see the consequence of sin all around us. Tragedy is around every corner. Yet, we also saw how God's character is marked by mercy. Through Jeremiah, He promised a future restoration and rescue. That rescue became a reality in the person of Jesus. In the powerful name of Jesus, you and I can experience mercy as well. As we experience the great mercy of Jesus, let us, like Jeremiah, share the good news of the Lord.

She is clothed with strength and dignity;
she can laugh at the days to come.

PROVERBS 31:25

Proverbs 31 Ministries is a nondenominational, nonprofit Christian ministry that seeks to lead women into a personal relationship with Christ. With Proverbs 31:10-31 as a guide, Proverbs 31 Ministries reaches women in the middle of their busy days through free devotions, daily radio messages, speaking events, conferences, resources, online Bible studies and training in the call to write, speak and lead others.

We are real women offering real-life solutions to those striving to maintain life's balance, in spite of today's hectic pace and cultural pull away from godly principles.

Wherever a woman may be on her spiritual journey, Proverbs 31 Ministries exists to be a trusted friend who understands the challenges she faces and walks by her side, encouraging her as she walks toward the heart of God.

Visit us online today at proverbs31.org!

Proverbs 31
MINISTRIES